GREEK MYTHOLOGY

ARTEMIS

BY HEATHER C. HUDAK

CONTENT CONSULTANT
ALISON C. TRAWEEK, PhD
ADJUNCT INSTRUCTOR OF GREEK AND ROMAN CLASSICS
TEMPLE UNIVERSITY

Kids Core
An Imprint of Abdo Publishing
abdobooks.com

abdobooks.com

Published by Abdo Publishing, a division of ABDO, PO Box 398166, Minneapolis, Minnesota 55439. Copyright © 2022 by Abdo Consulting Group, Inc. International copyrights reserved in all countries. No part of this book may be reproduced in any form without written permission from the publisher. Kids Core™ is a trademark and logo of Abdo Publishing.

Printed in the United States of America, North Mankato, Minnesota.
102021
012022

Cover Photo: Hoika Mikhail/Shutterstock Images
Interior Photos: Shutterstock Images, 4–5, 8, 12 (deer), 12 (Mount Olympus), 23, 28 (bottom), 29 (bottom); iStockphoto, 7, 10–11, 12 (bow and arrow), 14, 29 (top); Darko Mlinarevic/iStockphoto, 12 (Artemis); Christophel Fine Art/Universal Images Group/Getty Images, 16; Album/Alamy, 18; Anna Krivitskaya/Shutterstock Images, 20–21, 28 (top); Photo Researchers/Science History Images/Alamy, 22; Mondadori Portfolio/Hulton Fine Art Collection/Getty Images, 25; Painters/Alamy, 26

Editor: Alyssa Sorenson
Series Designer: Ryan Gale

Library of Congress Control Number: 2021941251

Publisher's Cataloging-in-Publication Data

Names: Hudak, Heather C., author.
Title: Artemis / by Heather C. Hudak
Description: Minneapolis, Minnesota : Abdo Publishing, 2022 | Series: Greek mythology | Includes online resources and index.
Identifiers: ISBN 9781532196744 (lib. bdg.) | ISBN 9781098218553 (ebook)
Subjects: LCSH: Artemis (Greek deity)--Juvenile literature. | Mythology, Greek--Juvenile literature. | Gods, Greek--Juvenile literature.
Classification: DDC 292--dc23

CONTENTS

CHAPTER 1
Mighty Artemis 4

CHAPTER 2
Goddess of the Hunt 10

CHAPTER 3
Respected and Worshipped 20

Legendary Facts 28
Glossary 30
Online Resources 31
Learn More 31
Index 32
About the Author 32

The Greek goddess Artemis knew how dangerous giants were.

CHAPTER **1**

MIGHTY ARTEMIS

Some ancient stories say giants once roamed Earth. Two of these giants were twin brothers. They were known as the Aloadae. The brothers were powerful. Everyone feared them, including the Olympian gods.

Some stories say the brothers wanted to destroy the gods' home. No one knew how to stop them except for a goddess named Artemis. She found out the brothers could be killed only by each other.

Artemis was the goddess of wild animals, the hunt, and childbirth. She had a special

Olympian Gods

The Olympians were important gods in Greek mythology. They were Artemis, Aphrodite, Apollo, Ares, Athena, Demeter, Dionysus, Hephaestus, Hera, Hermes, Hestia, Poseidon, and Zeus. Many of them ruled over Earth from the peak of Mount Olympus. Mount Olympus is a real place in Greece. But the ancient Greeks believed humans couldn't reach the spot where the gods lived.

Artemis was often associated with the forest.

power. She could change herself into an animal. One day, the giant brothers were out hunting. Artemis turned herself into a doe. She ran between the two giants. They threw their spears at her, but she ran off.

Some Greek myths talk about battles against monsters.

They struck each other instead. Both brothers died. Artemis had stopped the giants.

What Is Greek Mythology?

Ancient Greece was a **civilization** in southeastern Europe. It existed more than

2,000 years ago. The ancient Greeks were well-known for their **epics**. Many of these stories were about gods and goddesses. They rewarded people for being good. They also punished people if they behaved poorly. Stories about Greek gods, goddesses, monsters, and heroes are known as Greek mythology. Many myths were about a young goddess named Artemis.

> ### Further Evidence
> Look at the website below. Does it give any new evidence to support Chapter One?
>
> ### Artemis
> abdocorelibrary.com/artemis

Artemis's father, Zeus, was the king of the gods.

GODDESS OF THE HUNT

Artemis was one of Zeus's daughters. Leto was Artemis's mother. She was a Titan. The Titans were mighty gods. They ruled the world before Zeus and his siblings overthrew them.

Artemis Quick Facts

Parents
Leto and Zeus

Home
Mount Olympus

Goddess of
Wild animals, the hunt, and childbirth

Important Animals to Artemis
Deer and bears

Symbols
Bow and arrows and the moon

Friends
Nymphs, who were divine females that lived for a long time and were connected to nature

Many ancient Greeks knew the most important facts about Artemis.

Leto gave birth to Artemis on a small island in the Aegean Sea. It was painless and easy. But the birth of Artemis's twin, Apollo, was difficult for Leto. Artemis helped her mother. That's how Artemis became the goddess of childbirth. Ancient Greeks believed she helped women give birth. But she could also take their lives if she chose.

Who Was Apollo?

Apollo was a Greek god who represented many things, including music, healing, and archery. He often protected boys, but sometimes he would bring them diseases and death. In artwork, Apollo is often seen as young and handsome.

Some stories say Artemis watches over wild things growing in forests.

Artemis spent most of her time in nature. She loved forests, mountains, and **marshes**. She used her bow and arrows to hunt wild animals. But she also protected them, especially young ones. Artemis could turn herself and others into animals too.

Artemis was very powerful and **independent**. She never wanted to get married. However, she still punished people who broke their wedding vows. She rewarded those who kept them. Artemis also protected young girls until they got married. She could heal people, but she could bring death and disease too.

In some stories, Artemis, *top*, doesn't save Agamemnon's daughter, *middle*.

Conflicts with Others

Sometimes Artemis could be **vengeful**. One time, a man named Actaeon saw Artemis bathing in the woods. She found out and turned Actaeon into a stag. Then she sent his hunting dogs after him.

In another story, a king named Agamemnon was about to sail his ships to war. He said that he was a better hunter than Artemis. The goddess became angry. She made the wind stop so the king could not sail. He needed to make Artemis happy. He decided to **sacrifice** his daughter to the goddess. Artemis was pleased with this plan. But she decided to save the girl and take her away.

Many men went out to hunt the wild boar that Artemis sent.

Another myth talks about King Oeneus. He gave the first fruits of the land to the gods. One year, he forgot to include Artemis. The goddess was upset. She sent a large wild boar to attack the king's land. It destroyed everything in its path until it was hunted down.

PRIMARY SOURCE

A poet once wrote about Artemis's different interests:

> The goddess with a bold heart turns every way destroying the race of wild beasts: and when she is satisfied . . . she hangs up her curved bow and her arrows, and heads and leads the dances [in Delphi].

Source: "Hymn 27 to Artemis." *Perseus Digital Library*, n.d., perseus.tufts.edu. Accessed 20 July 2021.

Comparing Texts

Think about the quote. Does it support the information in this chapter? Or does it give a different perspective? Explain how in a few sentences.

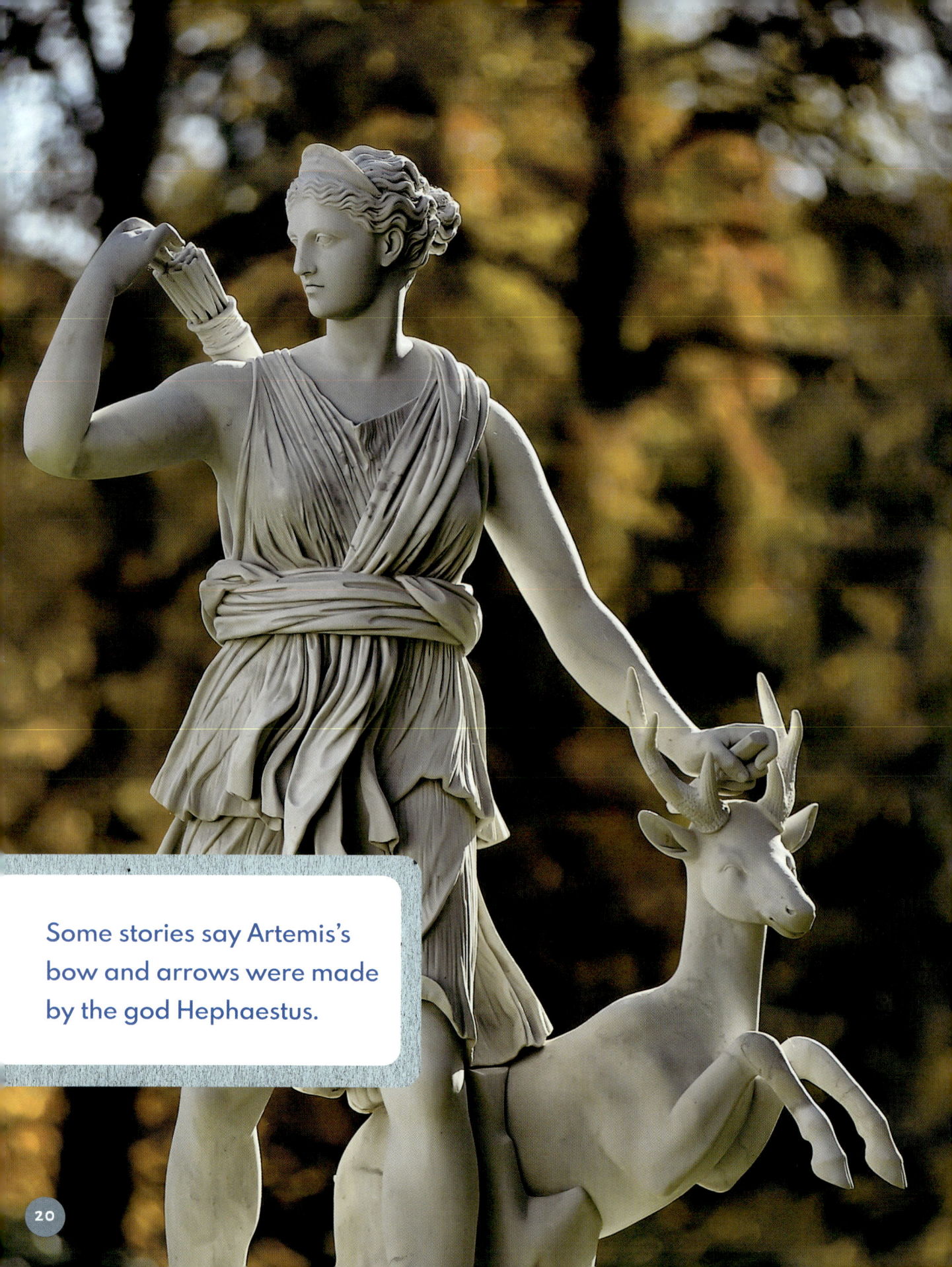

Some stories say Artemis's bow and arrows were made by the god Hephaestus.

CHAPTER **3**

RESPECTED AND WORSHIPPED

People all over ancient Greece worshipped Artemis. Pregnant women prayed to her for smooth childbirths. They brought gifts to **temples** after they gave birth. It was their way of thanking the goddess.

Artists imagine what the Temple of Artemis may have looked like in ancient times.

The ancient Greeks built many temples to honor Artemis. One of the best-known temples is in Ephesus. This is an area in modern-day Turkey. The temple was built around 550 BCE. People can see its ruins today.

Today, not much remains of the Temple of Artemis in Turkey.

In ancient times, every five years young girls visited a temple near Athens, Greece. They went there to honor Artemis. At the temple, people would sacrifice goats to make the goddess happy.

Artemis in Art

Artemis is pictured in many ancient Greek artworks, such as paintings and sculptures. She was thought to be a beautiful young woman. Artists sometimes showed her wearing a knee-length **tunic**. Artemis carried a bow and arrows or a spear. Hunting dogs or wild animals, such as deer, would be at her side.

The Artemis Program

The National Aeronautics and Space Administration (NASA) is a US government group. It studies space. NASA has a program called Artemis. The program will again send astronauts to explore the moon.

Some writers have called Artemis the mistress of animals.

Today, Artemis continues to live on in people's imaginations.

Some people linked Artemis with the moon and Apollo with the sun. In artwork, Artemis sometimes carries a torch. She may also wear a crown in the shape of the moon.

Artemis was a favorite goddess of the ancient Greeks. They believed she could help or hurt them. Myths about Artemis are thousands of years old. Many stories about this goddess are still told today.

Explore Online

Visit the website below. Does it give any new information about Artemis that wasn't in Chapter Three?

Artemis

abdocorelibrary.com/artemis

LEGENDARY FACTS

Artemis was the goddess of childbirth, wild animals, and the hunt. She could change herself into an animal if she wanted.

Artemis helped take down the mighty Aloadae giants.

Artemis loved spending time in nature. She often wandered around mountains, marshes, and forests.

Many ancient Greeks prayed to Artemis. They hoped she would help them with childbirth.

Glossary

civilization
a society that's organized and developed

epics
stories of great adventures, events, or fictional places

independent
free and not under the control of someone else

marshes
areas of soft, wet land

sacrifice
to offer something as a gift to a god or goddess

temple
a building used for worship

tunic
a simple, loose-fitting shirt that falls down to the knees and is belted at the waist

vengeful
feeling or showing a strong desire to get back at someone

Online Resources

To learn more about Artemis, visit our free resource websites below.

Visit **abdocorelibrary.com** or scan this QR code for free Common Core resources for teachers and students, including vetted activities, multimedia, and booklinks, for deeper subject comprehension.

Visit **abdobooklinks.com** or scan this QR code for free additional online weblinks for further learning. These links are routinely monitored and updated to provide the most current information available.

Learn More

Flynn, Sarah Wassner. *Greek Mythology*. National Geographic, 2018.

Hudak, Heather C. *Zeus*. Abdo, 2022.

Menzies, Jean. *Greek Myths*. DK, 2020.

Index

Actaeon, 17
Agamemnon, 17
animals, 6–7, 12, 15, 19, 24
Apollo, 6, 13, 27
Artemis program, 24

boar, 18
bow and arrows, 12, 15, 19, 24

childbirth, 6, 12–13, 21

giants, 5–8

Leto, 11–13

nature, 12, 15

sacrifice, 17, 23
spear, 7, 24

temple, 21–23
Titans, 11

Zeus, 6, 11–12

About the Author

Heather C. Hudak has written hundreds of books on all kinds of topics. She loves to travel when she's not writing. Hudak has visited about 60 countries. She has been to many ancient sites in Greece dedicated to Artemis and the Olympians.